No Quick Fix:
Fad Diets & Weight-Loss Miracles

D1501757

Understanding Obesity

No Quick Fix:
Fad Diets & Weight-Loss Miracles

Jean Ford with Autumn Libal

Mason Crest

Mason Crest
450 Parkway Drive, Suite D
Broomall, PA 19008
www.masoncrest.com

Printed in the United States of America.

Series ISBN: 978-1-4222-3056-5
ISBN: 978-1-4222-3065-7
ebook ISBN: 978-1-4222-8848-1

Cataloging-in-Publication Data on file with the Library of Congress.

Contents

KEY ICONS TO LOOK FOR:

Text-Dependent Questions: These questions send the reader back to the text for more careful attention to the evidence presented there.

Words to Understand: These words with their easy-to-understand definitions will increase the reader's understanding of the text, while building vocabulary skills.

Series Glossary of Key Terms: This back-of-the book glossary contains terminology used throughout this series. Words found here increase the reader's ability to read and comprehend higher-level books and articles in this field.

Research Projects: Readers are pointed toward areas of further inquiry connected to each chapter. Suggestions are provided for projects that encourage deeper research and analysis.

Sidebars: This boxed material within the main text allows readers to build knowledge, gain insights, explore possibilities, and broaden their perspectives by weaving together additional information to provide realistic and holistic perspectives.

Introduction

We as a society often reserve our harshest criticism for those conditions we understand the least. Such is the case with obesity. Obesity is a chronic and often-fatal disease that accounts for 300,000 deaths each year. It is second only to smoking as a cause of premature death in the United States. People suffering from obesity need understanding, support, and medical assistance. Yet what they often receive is scorn.

Today, children are the fastest growing segment of the obese population in the United States. This constitutes a public health crisis of enormous proportions. Living with childhood obesity affects self-esteem, employment, and attainment of higher education. But childhood obesity is much more than a social stigma. It has serious health consequences.

Childhood obesity increases the risk for poor health in adulthood and premature death. Depression, diabetes, asthma, gallstones, orthopedic diseases, and other obesity-related conditions are all on the rise in children. Over the last 20 years, more children are being diagnosed with type 2 diabetes—a leading cause of preventable blindness, kidney failure, heart disease, stroke, and amputations. Obesity is undoubtedly the most pressing nutritional disorder among young people today.

This series is an excellent first step toward understanding the obesity crisis and profiling approaches for remedying it. If we are to reverse obesity's current trend, there must be family, community, and national objectives promoting healthy eating and exercise. As a nation, we must demand broad-based public-health initiatives to limit TV watching, curtail junk food advertising toward children, and promote physical activity. More than rhetoric, these need to be our rallying cry. Anything short of this will eventually fail, and within our lifetime obesity will become the leading cause of death in the United States if not in the world.

Victor F. Garcia, M.D.
Founder, Bariatric Surgery Center
Cincinnati Children's Hospital Medical Center
Professor of Pediatrics and Surgery
School of Medicine
University of Cincinnati

Words to Understand

stigma: The disgrace attached to something seen as socially unacceptable.

type 2 diabetes: A disease caused by the lack of or inefficient use of insulin, usually occurring in adulthood, but being increasingly seen in teenagers and younger children.

osteoarthritis: A form of arthritis characterized by the gradual wearing away of the cartilage of the joints.

media: The methods of mass communication, including television, newspapers, and radio.

stereotypes: Oversimplified ideas held by one person or group about another person or group, often based on inaccurate and incomplete information.

Chapter 1

A Heavyweight Matchup: Our Bodies Versus the Diet Industry

- America's Obesity Crisis
- Body Mass Index
- The Diet Industry Weighs In

America's Obesity Crisis

In today's world, there are many things that demand our thoughts and attention. Our daily commitments to school, work, and family already occupy most of our time. Then there are broader concerns like events in our communities, challenges to our governments, or situations around the world. With so many obligations and issues vying for our attention, many important things can escape our notice. With our concerns pulled in so many directions, we may begin neglecting some of the things that are closest to us, particularly our own bodies and health.

Though many of us do not know it, Americans today are experiencing a health crisis. According to The Weight-control Information Network, an information service of the National Institute of Diabetes and Digestive and Kidney Disease (NIDDK), over two-thirds of America's adult population is overweight. One-third of all American adults are obese. But struggles with weight are not limited to adults. America's young people are also suffering like never before. Today, one out of three young people ages six to nineteen are overweight or obese.

For those who suffer with overweight and obesity, it is often their own feelings toward their physical appearance and the social **stigma** that they face that are most devastating. There are, however, many other reasons to be concerned about weight issues—reasons that have nothing to do with appearance.

Overweight and obesity carry huge short- and long-term health risks. In the short term, excess weight has impacts like decreasing one's fitness and energy levels, increasing cholesterol, elevating blood pressure, and negatively impacting mood. In the long term, excess weight increases one's risk of atherosclerosis (clogged arteries), **type 2 diabetes**, cancer, **osteoarthritis**, stroke, heart attack, and other debilitating and life-threatening conditions. Those are huge risks! Clearly, if a person is truly overweight, he needs to take action to protect his health. His life and longevity depend on it.

But how does a person know if he is truly overweight? American culture today is one that values thinness to the point of absurdity. Many people, looking at the skinny models and actors pictured in the **media**, assume that they in comparison must be overweight. This is plainly untrue! The images of starvation-thin models we see all around us are ridiculous and unachievable standards of beauty. Worse yet, being underweight (which one would have to be to conform to many beauty **stereotypes**) can be just as dangerous and unhealthy as being overweight or obese. So how do you know if your weight is a healthy one or not? Thankfully, there are reliable tools that can help you understand your weight and what it means.

Body Mass Index

One tool commonly used by doctors and laypeople alike to determine the meaning of one's body size is body mass index (BMI). BMI is simply a formula that uses your height and weight to estimate the amount of your body that is made up of fat. According to the National Institutes of Health (NIH), BMI is a reliable indicator of approximate total body fat, one element necessary to assess overall fitness. BMI is also a useful tool because you can calculate it yourself without the help of trained professionals. If you are under twenty, go to this website to determine your BMI using one of the charts: www.cdc.gov/healthyweight/assessing/bmi/childrens_bmi/about_childrens_bmi.html. If you are over twenty, you can calculate your BMI using one of the following formulas:

BMI = [weight in pounds ÷ (height in inches x height in inches)] x 703
or
BMI = weight in kilograms ÷ (height in meters x height in meters)

Here is an example for a person who is 5'3" tall (63") and weighs 120 pounds. The equation looks like this:

[120 ÷ (63 x 63)] x 703 = BMI
[120 ÷ (3969)] x 703 = BMI
.03 x 703 = BMI
.03 x 703 = 21.09

Once you determine your BMI, you can compare the result to government guidelines.

BMI Classifications According to the CDC

BMI	Classification
< 18.5	= Underweight
18.5 – 24.9	= Normal
25.0 – 29.9	= Overweight
30.0 and above	= Obese

Keep in mind that BMI is not the sole indicator of health, and it has definite limitations. For example, it often overestimates body fat in very muscular people and athletes. According to BMI alone, Arnold Schwarzenegger, Sylvester Stallone, and Jean-Claude Van Damme are all obese. Anyone can see these men are bigger than average, but their bulk does not come from fat, so using the term "obese" to describe their physiques is very misleading. On the other hand, the index can underestimate body fat in the elderly and others who have lost muscle mass. Lastly, BMI offers no means of measuring heart-healthiness such as blood pressure or cholesterol. Hence, it becomes

critical to understand that BMI is merely one tool most effectively applied in conjunction with other factors like diet, physical activity, waist circumference, blood pressure, cholesterol levels, and blood sugar.

Still Americans need realistic, impartial standards to guide them to better health, and BMI is one of the best and most objective standards. Its numbers generally don't lie (unless, of course, we fudge the data we enter into the formula!). Sadly for many Americans, calculating their BMI would indeed yield an overweight or obese result. There's no denying it: Obesity is a problem in twenty-first-century America. But we face another crisis as well—bad information and companies that exploit our weight woes for profit!

The Diet Industry Weighs In

Whether truly suffering from a weight problem or just believing they would look better if they lost

Make Connections: Fat Facts

Since the 1960s, obesity among American adults has more than doubled, increasing from 13.4 to 35.7 percent.

Overweight and obesity put people at higher risks of developing many different types of cancers, such as breast, colon, esophagus, and kidney cancer.
Obesity is the second-leading preventable cause of death.

weight, millions of Americans are desperately scrambling for weight-loss solutions. Literally thousands of weight-loss products, programs, and plans scream for our attention. America's weight crisis has spawned a multi-billion dollar industry. In 2010, Americans spend $61 billion on diet products, which is equal to $200 being spent on every man, woman, and child in the United States. The diet products consists of meals like Lean Cuisine® and NutriSystem®, and also of "miracle" drugs that are supposed to help people lose the pounds quickly. And yet, we're still getting fatter. Sadly, the vast majority of the diet industry is not part of the solution; it's part of the problem.

Who exactly are we talking about when we use the term "diet industry"? And more importantly, what is a "diet"? People may use these terms in different ways, but in this book, we define a "diet" as any program that for the purpose of weight loss modifies the type or amount of food consumed. However, we will not consider certain modifications (like reducing one's intake of salt, fat, or sugar; increasing one's intake of fiber; or increasing exercise) that are made for specific medical- or health-related goals (such as lowering cholesterol, reducing one's risk of developing diabetes, or lowering blood pressure) to be "diets." We will consider anyone who develops, manufactures, or markets weight-loss products to be part of the "diet industry."

In this book, you will learn the truth about the diet industry and all the "tried and true" weight-loss methods it hawks at the expense of your wallet and your health. Along the way, you will also learn why your focus should be good health, not weight loss, and what the best approach is for truly achieving that goal. Before we do that, however, let's examine why so many of us believe we need these weight-loss products and why we are so quick to swallow the diet industry's lies. To do so, we will examine how the popular media has influenced America and how the diet industry uses this influence to further its own profit-driven goals.

Text-Dependent Questions:

1. What is the "diet industry"?
2. What percentage of American adults are obese today?

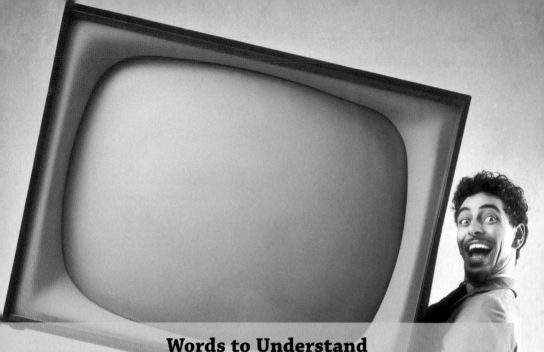

Words to Understand

altruistic: Unselfish.

psyche: Mental characteristics typical of a nation, a people, or a group.

wield: To have and be able to use power or authority.

Victorian: Something that relates to or is characteristic of the reign of Queen Victoria during the 1800s.

anorexia: An eating disorder characterized by a fear of being overweight and excessive dieting to the extreme of serious illness and sometimes death.

bulimia: An eating disorder characterized by periods of overeating followed by undereating, the use of laxatives, or self-induced vomiting.

industrialized: Adopted industrial methods of production and manufacturing, accompanied by growth in cities.

socioeconomic: Something that involves both social and economic factors.

cachet: A quality of distinction leading to admiration.

gluttony: The act of excessive eating or drinking.

personified: Seen as the perfect example of something.

rhetoric: The effective use of language (often fine-sounding but insincere) to persuade or influence people.

Chapter 2

The Media's Mark

The Power of the Media

"I was on a plane the morning *USA Today* headlines read, 'Coffee raises cholesterol.' No one drank coffee that trip. On another flight headlines claimed coffee might prevent cancer, and everyone ordered it. Then *Time* reported that vitamin C could prevent ulcers—in another article, it was reported in another sample that vitamin C prevented Alzheimer's—and everyone suddenly wanted orange juice. A few weeks later, yet another study suggested OJ causes heartburn, reflux disease, even esophageal cancer; and nobody wanted orange juice anymore. Now look what's happening to the bread industry. Roll-less hamburgers? Man, we're crazy."

The above quote by a Pennsylvania businessperson clearly illustrates the power the media can have on people's daily thoughts and actions. But the media's influence can be even more dramatic. For example, on October 30, 1938, many Americans tuned to a popular radio program featuring plays directed by Orson Welles. That evening, Halloween eve, the show performed an adaptation of a science-fiction novel *The War of the Worlds*, by H. G. Wells, in which Martians invade Earth. Welles made an important change, though, when adapting the book to radio. The plot was played out as a series of simulated, emergency news broadcasts ("on location" with fictionalized, but realistic sound effects), which interrupted "regular programming."

In one scene, a studio actor playing a newscaster reporting "live from the scene" described aliens emerging from a spacecraft. He reported in an appropriately halting and confused voice, "That face . . . it . . . it's indescribable. I can hardly force myself to keep looking at it. The eyes are black and gleam like a serpent. The mouth is v-shaped with saliva dripping from its rimless lips. . . . The thing is rising up! The crowd falls back; they've seen enough . . . I can't find words . . . I'm pulling the microphone with me as I talk. I'll have to stop the description until I find a new position. Hold on . . . ."

Welles's intention was simply to entertain, not to convince people that aliens were *actually* invading the Earth; there was even a disclaimer read saying that it was a radio drama. Nevertheless, many people bought it. They thought the Earth was genuinely under attack! Panic ensued. A portion of the listening audience hid in cellars, loaded their guns, flooded the streets, and even wrapped their heads in wet towels to protect against the invaders' poison gas. They *believed* the content of the broadcast simply because they heard it on their radios.

Lest you think blind trust of the media is limited to early twentieth-century audiences, jump ahead to April 1, 1996. Readers in five major U.S cities opened their newspapers that morning to full-page articles (actually paid advertisements) announcing Taco Bell's purchase of the Liberty Bell from the U.S. government. According to the article, the corporation claimed its motive behind the purchase was **altruistic**, to "help the national debt."

Indifferent to the April Fools' Day release date, hundreds of legitimate newspapers and television shows ran stories on the article's claims, and believing citizens flooded Liberty Bell National Park with phone calls to complain about the sale. Many Americans embraced the crazy story as true, despite common sense, because they saw it in the newspaper. A few hours later, Taco Bell's public relations firm announced the story was a hoax.

Two outrageous stories in the media. Two deceived audiences. One group unintentionally influenced; the other, intentionally fooled. In both examples, the media's power to impact the collective **psyche** of a nation is undeniable.

The War of the Worlds fiasco is undoubtedly the most infamous example of our media's ability to influence audiences en masse. Now, spin artists and marketers utilize that ability every day to influence our opinions and get into our pockets.

Granted, much of what we encounter in the media is factual, objective, and accurate. Responsible journalists and even responsible advertisers do exist. Many reports, though, sensationalize, exaggerate, or deliberately slant

material to further a hidden agenda, particularly when dollars are at stake. Whatever the motive, the information taints our perceptions.

The fashion and diet industries **wield** this power perhaps most intensely of all industries. During the last century, mainstream media has dictated what we believe about ourselves, our bodies, fitness, and health. Whether we admit to it or not, many of us have bought every message hook, line, and sinker. And it's cost us. Let's take a look.

A Changing Nation

In the mid-1800s, the principal causes of death and disability among Americans were infectious diseases linked partly to poor or inadequate food intake. So the goals of health officials and the food industry were the same: encourage people to eat more of all kinds of foods. In fact, physicians instructed the masses to *gain* weight. Full, curvy bodies became synonymous with health and wealth; stoutness in both men and women was a symbol of prosperity, a sign one could afford to eat well. Skinny, bony bodies remained indicative of poverty and malnutrition. Plump, round, **Victorian** figures were in, and heavy was "sexy." A good layer of abdominal and hip fat was thought to mean a woman was more fertile, able to successfully endure childbirth, and better equipped to fight off infectious disease—all desirable traits. Men considered chubby arms and cheeks beautiful. Gaunt, hollow looks were "low class."

What happened? How did America move from "soft and bulky is beautiful" to twenty-first-century advertising campaigns featuring "heroin-chic" models? (Ironically, many such ads run side-by-side with articles on **anorexia** and **bulimia**.)

Over the years, America has changed a lot, and so have our attitudes toward beauty. It is quite common for whole societies to admire and value what its wealthiest members have and to devalue and scorn the little that the poor have. Well, when food was hard to come by and only the wealthiest

members of society could get enough of it to be plump, extra pounds were desirable and considered beautiful. Over the last century, however, America **industrialized**. New technologies improved people's lives on nearly all levels of the **socioeconomic** scale. Advances in farming techniques, fertilizers, pesticides, transportation, storage, and countless other areas made food more plentiful, cheaper, and more accessible than ever before. New jobs in the industrial economy meant more people were earning money, and therefore they were able to purchase food instead of forced to grow it themselves. All this meant was that it suddenly wasn't so difficult to have enough to eat, or even to gain a few extra pounds. Plumpness was no longer the privilege of the rich, and it therefore began to lose its mystique and **cachet**.

Suddenly anyone could be plump, even those of modest means. The elite no longer had exclusive rights to fat, and well-to-do Americans wanted to re-distinguish themselves from the masses. The upper class controlled the media and advertising, as it often does, hence it controlled much of what the populace saw and read. Soon it was chic to be thin—as seen in the flat, angular, "flapper" look of the 1920s—and fat became ordinary. The status symbols reversed.

Changes in American attitudes toward beauty, however, haven't just been about class relationships. There have been other important factors as well, such as Puritan philosophies and ethics. The Puritans, a Protestant religious group that was very influential in early America, preached strict morality and a "pure" lifestyle. In their view, a pure and moral life was one devoid of earthly and bodily pleasures. A life of self-sacrifice on earth was believed to make one more worthy of heaven. Ben Franklin was expressing his Puritan philosophies when he stated, "Eat for necessity, not pleasure." According to this philosophy, **gluttony** was one of many sins relating to physical pleasure. Becoming plump, therefore, was a sure sign that one was being gluttonous and therefore sinful.

By the 1920s, many Americans believed thinness was not only a sign of affluence, but of superior morality. Society soon viewed "giving in to the flesh" (indulging the body's cravings) as immoral and offensive to God.

Certainly not everyone in twentieth-century America subscribed to Puritan philosophies. Nevertheless, these beliefs did contribute to an overall attitude that thinness was preferable to plumpness and even that people who were overweight were somehow worse or less valuable than people who were thin. Consider this passage from an early New York City reader: "Do not eat more than is necessary. Persons who eat too much are gluttons. They are stupid, and heavy, and idle."

There were a few voices, however, who spoke out against the trend toward thinness. In a 1926 issue of *Cosmopolitan*, Dr.

> *"How decisively even ten or fifteen extra pounds detract from one's appearance and make the most expensive gown dowdy. A youthful, slender figure means everything today."*
> —A 1930s advertisement published in *Cosmopolitan*

Woods Hutchinson, a medical professor, writer, and eventual president of the American Academy of Medicine wrote, "The longed-for slender and boyish figure is becoming a menace, not only to the present, but to future generations." If only he knew how prophetic his words would become.

Signs of the Times

Miss America winners from 1922 to 1999 illustrate America's trend toward thinness perfectly. These cultural icons dropped bulk steadily from the 1920s. With each decade, winners' weights gradually fell from within the healthy "normal" range (a BMI of twenty to twenty-five) to a BMI low of 16.9. Since the 1960s, nearly all winners have had BMIs below 18.5, the point at which the World Health Organization considers a person "undernourished."

Industrialization and a Puritan ethic certainly weren't the last or even the most influential factors in America's changing attitudes toward beauty. The last half of the twentieth century saw the thin-is-in mentality evolve to its extreme. New media like television and movies created a whole new elite class everyone wanted to emulate: The Stars. Hollywood and New York accelerated the thinness movement with angular stars like Audrey Hepburn and Brigitte Bardot. Even the toy industry promoted the "ideal"; Barbie®'s waist was freakishly thin. Then a young British teen, Lesley Hornby, **personified** and cemented the movement. At five-feet, four-inches tall and just ninety pounds, high-school classmates nicknamed her "Sticks" for her long, scrawny legs. (It wasn't meant as a compliment.) In 1966, the media discovered her, and we came to know this frail creature as Twiggy. This time, the compliment was clear, and emaciation became vogue overnight.

Today we live in a world altogether different from the nineteenth-century-America where plump was beautiful. Gone are many infectious diseases like tuberculosis, diphtheria, and cholera—all associated with thinness and frailty—that were once the leading causes of death. People no longer need extra layers of fat to survive the ravages of these diseases. Instead, obesity-related ailments like heart disease have replaced infectious disease as the number-one cause of death in America. Gone too are the days of widespread hunger. Today, you don't need lots of money to become overweight. On the contrary, people spend huge amounts of money to get thin. On top of it all, we have access to media (and therefore are vulnerable to its messages) like never before. The diet industry has struck gold.

Media World

In 1996 Alicia Silverstone, the slim, teenage movie star of *Batman* fame, appeared on the Academy Awards and suddenly found herself the target of vicious jokes and criticism. The reason? She had gained ten pounds since her last movie (for which she probably *lost* weight). The press mercilessly ridiculed her for days. "Batman and Fatgirl," "More Babe Than Babe," and "Look out Batman, Here Comes Buttgirl!" screamed the headlines. Silverstone's director responded with indignation. "What did this child do? Have a couple of pizzas? The news coverage was outrageous, judgmental, and cruel!"

Why talk about the power of the media? Why examine the history of U.S. body image? Before we can effectively explore the diet industry, we must understand why so many of us think it's so important to be, not healthy, but thin. After all, that's why we're dieting, and intentionally losing weight is a relatively new phenomenon in human history. Think about it: What message did the press's criticism of Silverstone send to other teens?

At no other time in history has a culture's obsession with thinness been more severe and extreme. Unnatural thinness is now widely encouraged and in some circles even considered healthy. Men and women on camera are getting thinner and thinner. Caved-in stomachs, bony clavicles,

Make Connections: A Deadly Shift

According to the National Center for Health Statistics, the top three killers in the United States in 1900 and 2010 were:

1900	*2010*
Tuberculosis	Heart Disease
Pneumonia	Cancer
Diarrheal Diseases	Stroke

protruding hipbones, and frighteningly skeletal faces—all historically images of famine or abuse—now grace magazine covers and advertisements as normal and desirable.

Research Project

Go to the library and look at art books or go online and search for artwork from the past. See if you can find pictures of women from the 1500s, 1600s, the 1700s, the 1800s, and the 1900s. Describe what was apparently considered beautiful in terms of body type for each century. How has our concept of beauty changed over the centuries? Why do you think this is?

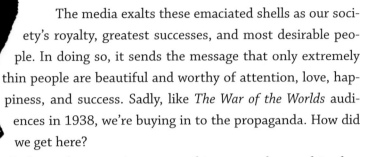

The media exalts these emaciated shells as our society's royalty, greatest successes, and most desirable people. In doing so, it sends the message that only extremely thin people are beautiful and worthy of attention, love, happiness, and success. Sadly, like *The War of the Worlds* audiences in 1938, we're buying in to the propaganda. How did we get here?

Perhaps the most important thing to understand is that those who stand to profit from shaping our views use the popular media as a marketing tool. Companies who have something to sell need access to you, and the popular media is where they gain that access. Whether their pitch is a straightforward advertisement or a cleverly hidden product placement, their sole goal is to get you not only to want their product but to believe you *need* it. How? Advertisers know we're

Even soft-drink giant Coca-Cola Company has used the "thin-is-in" image to market its products. In a past marketing campaign for Diet Sprite, marketing execs chose to use a bony girl listlessly sipping her diet drink while boasting her nickname was "Skeleton." Public outcry forced the company to pull the ad.

Text-Dependent Questions:

1. Describe two historical cases where people believed a false story simply because it was broadcast by the media.
2. What kind of body was considered healthy in the 1800s?
3. Explain how wealth is related to a culture's sense of what is attractive in terms of thinness and obesity.
4. What were the top three fatal diseases in 1900? What were they in 2010?

preoccupied with physique, and they exploit this fact by reinforcing the idea that something is wrong with our bodies, that we are not okay as we are. And it's not just clothing and cosmetic companies. The food and diet industries are also in on the action. Don't be fooled by **rhetoric**. These companies generally are not concerned with our health at all; they want to sell their products. Period. And billions of dollars are at stake.

Words to Understand

pariahs: People who are hated and avoided by other people.

inherently: Characteristically part of something else to the extent that one cannot be considered separate from the other.

Chapter 3

The Diet Industry: Profiting from Our Health

- Preying on Emotions

- The True Bottom Line

Preying on Emotions

Laura, from Pennsylvania, is fifteen. Friends and family describe her as smart, popular, pretty, happy, and very perceptive. She's fun to be around. Her body is already slim, but her mind is obsessed with perfecting it. "Every day at school, someone tells me I have a great body. Other kids compliment me all the time, but I still weigh myself three times a day so the scale doesn't creep up. It should be creeping down. Not that I think I'm fat or anything. It's just that if I weighed five pounds less, I'd be closer to perfect and I'd respect myself more."

Merryl Bear, coordinator of the National Eating Disorder Information Center in Toronto, Ontario, is very familiar with statements like Laura's. Bear explains, "Because our society is so focused on appearance, body image becomes central to our feelings of self-esteem and self-worth." Consequently, we'll do anything to "perfect" our bodies and feel better about ourselves.

Consider these facts: According to one study done in 2012, 23 percent of women stated that they were on a diet. Of those women, about one-third stated that they were following a dieting plan of their own making. Another study done by the International Food Council Foundation had that 55 percent of people are trying to lose some weight, and that almost 60 percent of adults wish to lose at least twenty pounds. Twenty-six percent of dieters said that they followed the diet for less than a month, 36 percent followed a diet for one to six months, 11 percent followed a diet for one year, and 27 percent followed a diet for more than a year.

Many high school girls say they are terrified of being overweight. They are well aware of the stigma of obesity (even when they don't need to lose weight) and fear becoming **pariahs**. The peer pressure is almost unbearable. According to Frances M. Berg in her book *Children and Teens Afraid to Eat*, a recent study of New York high school girls revealed that 70 percent of

Make Connections: Medical Research

When a doctor or scientist makes a discovery, others in the field do not automatically accept it without question. The researcher submits the findings to other doctors and scientists for comment and to see if others can duplicate her results. One of the ways that information is submitted for criticism and additional discovery is through the *Journal of the American Medical Association* (*JAMA*), one of the most prestigious professional journals in the field of medicine. First published in 1883, *JAMA* is the professional journal of the American Medical Association and is published weekly. Before an article is accepted for publication, it goes through a peer-review process where others knowledgeable in the area critique it and make suggestions for further study. Once published, other researchers have the opportunity to examine the study, perform their own studies, and respond—positively or negatively—to the original report. In this way, the medical knowledge base is expanded.

Doctors and scientists are not the only ones who benefit from reading *JAMA*. There are articles for patients and others interested in nonclinical studies and reports.

high school females had tried to diet at least once. Twenty percent of under-weight girls, 32 percent of normal-weight girls, and 54 percent of overweight girls were currently dieting.

A similar survey in Cleveland high schools found that 70 percent of white girls and 60 percent of African American girls had lost five pounds or more in a weight-loss attempt. Most tried more dangerous methods at least once, including semi-starvation, fasting, vomiting, diuretics, fad diets, even smoking.

The "something's wrong with you unless you're thin" message impacts boys, too, perhaps most intensely through peers. Author Dan Davis writes in

Radiance, "My stomach still knots when I remember the echoes from my youth: 'I don't want you on my team.' 'Fat tub!' 'Your belly looks like a water-melon.' I'll carry the scars to my grave, but today's kids have it worse."

But Americans were not always so diet obsessed. In 1964, a Louis Harris Poll indicated only 15 percent of adult Americans were dieting at any given time. Fifteen percent up to 55 percent in just thirty years—that's a huge increase! What was a $120 million diet industry just years ago is now a $55 billion industry—according to CNBC—and as of 2010, $40 million of that was being spent by Americans.

The True Bottom Line

As more Americans have become overweight, people and companies have seen the enormous potential to build a market on this health crisis. But is this **inherently** bad? After all, overweight and obesity (whether or not we care about conforming to certain beauty standards) are serious problems. So if someone has a product that could alleviate these problems, why shouldn't that person or company make the product available to the public and make a profit to boot? If the diet industry can improve people's health, how can it possibly be a bad thing?

But here's the key question: Is the diet industry helping anyone? Are those products benefiting our health? For the billions of dollars Americans are spending each year, is anyone losing weight? And perhaps most importantly, would people in the diet industry intentionally deceive us by promoting products they know won't improve our health just to make a buck?

Here's the bottom line: If diets really worked, we'd all go on *one* diet *one* time and never have to lose weight again. (And the one program that *did* work would drive all the others and eventually itself out of business!) Then all the economic ventures that ride on the coattails of the diet industry—all diet foods, weight-loss magazines, diet clubs, self-help weight-loss books—would wither up and fade away. The diet industry's mere existence proves that diets do not work. Studies show that in 2011 alone, people on diets *gained* more weight than those who never dieted at all. In fact, according to the NPD Group, a market research company, dieters are giving up on diets more quickly than they did in previous years. Clearly diets don't work, or we'd never have to diet again.

So how can the diet industry survive and even grow by leaps and bounds? Because there's a catch: time. Within five years, perhaps more than 95 percent of dieters regain all the weight they lost (and many gain back even more). In the short term, however, just about any diet can cause a

Make Connections: A Paradox

By now you may be wondering, if Americans are so image conscious and value thinness so much, why are we becoming increasingly overweight and obese? It's an interesting paradox, isn't it? There are many influences contributing to our collective weight gain, but some of the biggest are changes in our eating habits and lifestyles. Today, Americans eat more prepackaged, highly processed, and fast foods than ever before (foods that are usually high in Calories, fat, salt, and sugar). At the same time, we are more sedentary than we have ever been. Between cars for transportation (instead of our feet or bikes), hours seated at desks, and televisions and computers for entertainment, we rarely engage in the physical activities that used to be a daily and necessary part of life.

Research Project

Go online and do a search for the word "diet." How many results come up? List the weight-loss plans you see just on the first page. Then click on each one to find out what each diet involves and what it promises.

Text-Dependent Questions:

1. What is evidence that diets don't work?
2. Explain what "yo-yo dieting" is.

brief, minimal weight loss. Even if all that is lost is water and no fat is truly burned, a quick drop of five or ten pounds can be enough hope to keep a desperate dieter coming back for more. These temporary, rapid weight losses followed by the inevitable weight gain, lead to a cycle called "yo-yo" dieting. It's on this cycle that the diet industry survives and thrives.

There are hundreds of diets out there for us to choose from, and each has a slightly different twist. Some recommend eliminating certain foods, others extol the benefits of a single food, and a few prescribe specific food combinations. Almost all work—for a time. Why? Because in the end, most modified eating programs, regardless of method, decrease total Calorie intake (we just don't know it), and, for the most part, weight loss demands fewer Calories "in" than Calories "burned."

While Calorie reduction can cause weight loss, simple Calorie reduction is not the answer to good health. In the rest of this book, we will examine types of diet programs and explore their legitimacy not by asking whether they will cause weight loss but by asking, "Will they make us healthy?" Before we can do this, however, we must know what our bodies need to be healthy.

Words to Understand

unbiased: Fair and impartial.
colon cancer: Cancer of the lower part of the intestine.
insulin: The hormone that regulates the body's blood-sugar level.
plaque: A deposit on the inner wall of an artery.
lard: White, soft, rendered pork fat used in cooking and baking and in some ointments and perfumes.
legumes: Seeds or pods used as food.

Chapter 4

What Our Bodies Really Need

Fuel for the Body's Engine

The human body is like a car. Cars need fuel to run and a variety of additives like oil, coolant, and lubricants to perform optimally. Similarly, your body needs fuel, or Calories, and a variety of nutrients to function healthfully.

A Calorie is a unit of energy. When we talk about the number of Calories in food, we talk about Calories with a capital "C." This type of Calorie is a kilocalorie or large calorie. It is the amount of energy needed to raise the temperature of one kilogram of water (approximately one liter or 4 and 1/4 cups) one degree Celsius. In areas of science like physics or chemistry that use very small measurements, one might discuss calories with a lowercase "c." This is a small calorie and is equivalent to the amount of heat it takes to raise one gram of water (approximately one millimeter or twenty drops from an eye dropper) one degree Celsius. There are 1,000 small calories in every food Calorie.

The number of Calories in any given food is the measure of potential energy the food contains, and different types of food have different amounts of potential energy. One gram of carbohydrates has four Calories, one gram of protein also has four Calories, and one gram of fat has nine Calories. Protein, carbohydrates, and fats are the building blocks of all foods. If you know how much of each block is in a particular food, then you know how many Calories, or how much energy, that food contains.

We burn Calories constantly. Every movement of our bodies requires energy in the form of Calories. Blinking our eyes, sneezing, breathing, walking, even chewing all consume Calories to varying extents. Our living, then, depends on a constant cycle of putting Calories in (via food), using that energy, then replenishing Calorie stores, much like we exhaust gas in our cars and refuel before driving farther. Since we're constantly burning energy, we need to eat regularly to function.

Our bodies need a constant supply of energy to keep our hearts pumping, limbs moving, brains thinking, and systems working. This, however, does not mean that we can take in a limitless supply of energy. If you take in more Calories in a day than you use up, you will have a *positive caloric balance*. The extra Calories will be stored as fat for use at a later time. (An accumulation of 3,500 surplus Calories becomes one pound of fat.) This is not bad, because a few days later, you might take in fewer Calories than you use in the day resulting in a *negative caloric balance*. In this event, your body will dip into its fat stores to get the energy it needs. (The ratio is the same: 3,500 more Calories burned uses one pound of stored fat.) However, if you end each day with a positive caloric balance and this pattern continues over a significant period of time, overweight and obesity can result. Similarly, if you regularly end each day with a negative caloric balance, malnourishment (or worse) can occur.

So how many Calories do you need each day to maintain health and a stable body weight? That number actually varies with each person. Two thousand is the most frequently cited number of Calories an average person needs in one day, but your body might actually require more or less. Height, weight, gender, and age all affect individual energy requirements, but three main factors carry the most influence: basal metabolic rate (BMR), physical activity, and the thermic effect of food.

Our Caloric Needs

Let's start with BMR. A person's BMR is the amount of energy her body needs to function at rest. This energy accounts for 60 to 75 percent of Calories burned in one day and includes the energy it takes to maintain body temperature and keep the heart beating, lungs breathing, and kidneys functioning. You can estimate your BMR using the Harris-Benedict Formula:

Adult Male = 66 + (6.3 x weight in pounds) + (12.9 x height in inches) – (6.8 x age in years)

Adult Female = 655 + (4.3 x weight in pounds) + (4.7 x height in inches) – (4.7 x age in years)

The second factor in determining daily caloric need is physical activity. Physical activity consumes the next-highest number of Calories, second only to at-rest demands. Every time you move, you are burning Calories on top of those required by your BMR. The more intense the activity, the more Calories will be burned. For example, you burn more Calories while running than you do while walking. The specific number of Calories a person burns performing any given activity, however, depends on additional factors like body weight and body fat percentage. For example, a larger person or person with a higher percentage of lean tissue to fat tissue will burn more Calories than a smaller person or a person with a lower percentage of lean tissue to fat tissue will burn performing the same activity. By examining the Calories at Work chart, you can get an idea of the impact body size has on the rate at which Calories are burned.

The third factor in tallying caloric need is the thermic effect of food, or the amount of energy your body uses to digest it. Digestion, like every other bodily process, requires energy. So you have to actually burn Calories to access the Calories in the food you've just eaten! To calculate the number of Calories you expend digesting food, simply multiply your daily Calorie intake by 10 percent. This will give you a general estimate. For example, if you take in 2,000 Calories each day, multiply 2,000 by .10. The answer, 200, is the number of Calories you burn just to digest the 2,000 Calories you took in.

If you add the results of these three calculations together, you will have a good estimate of the total number of Calories your body needs to function well throughout one day. A common myth about Calories is that weight gain or loss depends on where a Calorie originates. This is untrue. In terms of energy, and if we're only talking about *weight*, a Calorie is a Calorie is a Calorie.

CALORIES AT WORK			
Activity (1 Hour)	130lbs.	155lbs.	180lbs.
Aerobics (general)	384	457	531
Backpacking, hiking with pack	413	493	572
Badminton	266	317	368
Ballroom dancing (slow)	177	211	245
Ballroom dancing (fast)	325	387	449
Basketball (game)	472	563	654
Bowling	177	211	245
Boxing (punching bag)	354	422	490
Circuit training	472	563	654
Construction (outdoor)	325	387	449
Croquet	148	176	204
Cycling (leisure, <10 mph)	236	281	327
Cycling (light, 10-11.9 mph)	354	422	490
Cycling (moderate, 12-13.9 mph)	472	563	654
Cycling (racing, 16-19mph)	708	844	981
Darts	148	176	204
Fencing	354	422	490
Fishing (general)	177	211	245
Flag Football	472	563	654
Football (competitive)	531	633	735
Frisbee (general)	177	211	245
Frisbee (ultimate)	472	563	654
Gardening (general)	236	281	327
General Cleaning	207	246	286
Golf (miniature)	177	211	245
Golf (walking and carrying clubs)	266	317	368

A fat Calorie is no different than a protein Calorie or a carbohydrate Calorie. They are simply units of energy. Weight maintenance, gain, and loss, therefore, depend on very simple formulas. If we burn off the Calories we eat, we'll maintain our weight; if we burn more than we eat, we'll lose weight; if we burn less than we eat, we'll gain weight. But, if we're talking *nutrition* and *health*, the source of Calories definitely matters.

Nutrition and Health

When it comes to nutrition, there are all kinds of messages out there in the media. Be careful! Some of this information comes from reliable, **unbiased** sources and is based on sound scientific evidence. Other information is gathered, manipulated, and presented by people who hope to profit from your decisions. The truth is that every day your body needs energy and nutrients from a variety of sources, and few foods can be labeled all bad or all good. To begin understanding the importance of good nutrition, let's look at the basics: carbohydrates, fats, and proteins.

Carbohydrates

Carbohydrates are sugars, and they are found in numerous foods such as grain products, fruits, vegetables, and candy. According to the Group Health website, between 50 and 60 percent of your daily Calories should come from carbohydrates. Not all carbohydrates, however, are the same, and some are much better for you than others. The healthiest carbohydrates are complex carbohydrates. They are found in whole-grain foods like whole wheat bread, long-grain brown rice, and oatmeal and in many vegetables and fruits.

Make Connections: Fiber

Fiber is a complex carbohydrate that your body cannot break down. Therefore, fiber does not provide you with energy. The job fiber does in your body, however, is still essential for good health. Fiber does its work in the digestive tract. Here, it keeps food moving through your intestines and back out of your body. On its way, fiber soaks up fat, cholesterol, and naturally and artificially occurring toxins that are floating around in your intestines. If there were no fiber in your system, these undesirables could be absorbed into your body where they could contribute to conditions like heart disease. Or toxins could remain in your intestines for long periods of time, which might be a contributing factor to the development of **colon cancer**. Lack of fiber can also cause unpleasant constipation—when waste backs up in the intestines. For all these reasons, The American Dietetic Association recommends adults get an average of 20 to 35 grams of fiber every day. Currently American adults get an average of 5 to 14 grams per day. Foods that are high in fiber include whole oats, long-grain brown rice, beans, broccoli, apples, figs, prunes, leafy-green vegetables, and fruit and vegetable skins.

To figure out how many grams of carbohydrates you should eat each day, multiply the number of Calories you need by .50. Divide the result by four (the number of Calories in a gram of carbohydrate). This gives you the low-end of your necessary carbohydrate intake. Now multiply the number of Calories by .60, and divide the answer by four. This gives you the high-end of your necessary carbohydrate intake. Here is an example for a person who requires 2,200 Calories each day:

(2200 Calories x .50) / 4 Calories per gram of carbohydrates = 275 grams
(2200 Calories x .60) / 4 Calories per gram of carbohydrates = 330 grams

A person who requires 2,200 Calories should eat approximately 275 to 330 grams of carbohydrates (mostly complex) every day.

Complex carbohydrates take a long time for your body to break down and therefore supply your body with a sustained source of energy. Complex carbohydrates are also important because they are excellent sources of essential nutrients like vitamins, minerals, and fiber.

Whereas complex carbohydrates should be plentiful in your diet, simple carbohydrates such as sugar and highly refined grain products (like white bread and white rice) should make up a very small portion of your carbohydrate intake. Instead of being broken down slowly, simple carbohydrates break down all at once, flooding your body with sugar. A slow release of sugar is essential for sustained energy. A flood of sugar can overwhelm your system. When you eat lots of sugar, your body goes into **insulin**-production overdrive. The insulin pulls the sugar into your cells, which may cause you to experience a "sugar rush," or sudden surge of energy. Usually, however, your body can't burn this flood of sugar fast enough, so it stores the excess sugar as fat—your body's energy storehouse. Many simple carbohydrates are packed with Calories but are devoid of fiber and other nutrients; they are high-Calorie foods, but their Calories are "empty."

Fats

Fats, the most concentrated form of food energy, have a bad reputation. Contrary to popular belief, however, fats (especially certain types of fats) are necessary for good health. Fat is an essential part of many body tissues, is necessary for proper nervous system function, and transports certain vitamins around the body. The trick is to know which types of fats you should be eating and in what amounts.

According to the National Academy of Sciences, about 20 to 35 percent of your Calories should come from fats. Each gram of fat you consume contains nine Calories. That's more than twice the amount of energy contained in a gram of carbohydrates or proteins, so it takes far fewer grams of fat to give

you a high dose of Calories, one reason why fats contribute so readily to weight gain.

So how can you eat fats in a healthy and responsible way? They key is to know what type of fat you're eating. The three most important categories of fats are unsaturated, saturated, and trans fat. Unsaturated fats are liquid at room temperature. Common examples are olive and vegetable oils. Saturated fats are solid at room temperature. Butter is an example of a saturated fat. Trans fats are unsaturated fats that have undergone a chemical process called hydrogenation to make them solid at room temperature. Margarine and vegetable shortening are the most common examples of trans fats.

Of these three fat categories, one is safe and two are not. The key to which is which is cholesterol. Cholesterol is an essential part of cell membranes and nervous system tissues, but too much cholesterol can be dangerous . . . even deadly. Your body produces its own cholesterol, so when you ingest too much of it, the excess can build up on your artery walls. Eventually, this **plaque** can block the artery.

But the story becomes still more complicated, because just as there are "bad" and "good" fats, so too is there "bad" and "good" cholesterol. The "bad" cholesterol is *low-density lipoproteins* (LDL). This is the type of cholesterol that becomes artery-clogging plaque. Luckily, however, there is something called *high-density lipoproteins* (HDL)—the "good" cholesterol. Each HDL molecule has three binding sites—places where the LDL cholesterol latches on. When an LDL molecule is bound up by an HDL molecule, it is no longer free to stick to the artery wall and is instead flushed from the body. A problem occurs when you have too much LDL cholesterol and not enough HDL cholesterol to bind with it. So what determines whether a fat is considered "bad" or "good" is what type of cholesterol it contains or how it influences the cholesterol ratios in your body.

Saturated fats come mostly from animals and should be eaten in moderation because they contain cholesterol and will increase the amount of LDL cholesterol in your blood. According to the American Heart Association, you should limit your saturated fat intake to less than 7 percent of your total daily calories.

You can increase your levels of good cholesterol (HDL) by eating certain unsaturated fats. Unsaturated fats come in two forms, monounsaturated and polyunsaturated. Foods like avocados and olive oil are high in monoun-

You should consume less than 200 milligrams of cholesterol each day.

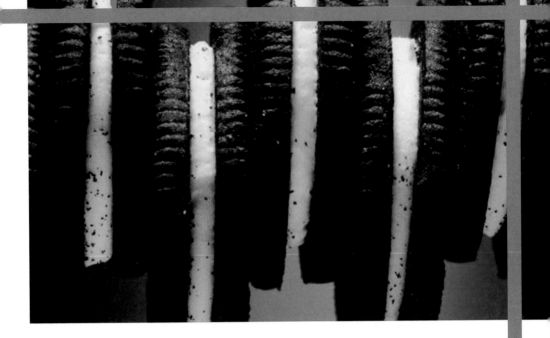

saturated fats, while foods like some grains, nuts, and fish are high in polyunsaturated fats. Polyunsaturated fats, especially those found in certain fish including salmon, lake trout, tuna, and mackerel, contain a high percentage of HDL cholesterol. However, despite the fact that unsaturated fats are good for you, they must be consumed in moderate amounts because they contain a large number of Calories. If eaten in excess, these fat Calories quickly contribute to weight gain.

Perhaps the unhealthiest form of fat is trans fat. For many years, people believed that trans fats were healthier than saturated fats. It was this belief that over the decades led to a massive, nationwide switch from butter to margarine and from **lard** to vegetable shortening. Now we know that we were very wrong. Trans fats also cause LDL cholesterol increases in the body. Furthermore, some studies suggest trans fats may be even more difficult for your body to break down than saturated fats. Some trans fats do occur in nature, mostly in animal products like red meat and dairy products, but your highest sources of trans fats are foods—like most crackers, cookies, cereals, and margarines—containing hydrogenated or partially hydrogenated vegetable oils.

Make Connections: Fat

To find out how many grams of fat you require each day, multiply the number of Calories you need by .20. Divide the resulting number by nine (the number of Calories in each gram of fat. The answer gives you the low-end of your necessary fat intake. Then multiply your daily Calories by .35, and divide the resulting number by nine. This gives you the high-end of your acceptable fat intake. Here is the formula for a person who requires 2,200 Calories each day:

(2200 Calories x .20) ÷ 9 Calories per gram of fat
   = 48.8 grams of fat
(2200 Calories x .35) ÷ 9 Calories per gram of fat
   = 85.5 grams of fat

A person who needs 2,200 Calories each day should consume approximately 48.8 to 85.5 grams of fat (less than 20 to 25 grams of it from saturated fat).

Protein

According to the Centers for Disease Control and Prevention, protein should account for 10 to 35 percent of your daily Calories. Protein, however, isn't just important for the caloric energy it gives you. It is also a major building block for your body. Without protein, you could not build or repair your muscles and other bodily tissues.

Contrary to much popular belief, protein actually comes from many sources (not just from meat). Most grains, nuts, and **legumes** are good sources of protein, and even many fruits and vegetables contain amino acids (the building blocks of protein). When you eat meat, dairy, and eggs, you ingest complete forms of protein, but you can also get all the amino acids necessary for your body to manufacture its own complete proteins by eating a wide variety of plant products. When you eat meat as your main source of protein, you also add a lot of fat and Calories to your diet. If this is a concern for you, you can decrease your caloric and fat intake and still get all the protein you need by replacing some of your meat and dairy with a variety of fruits, vegetables, grains, and legumes. Nuts are also a good source of protein, but like meat, they are high in fat and Calories. Nevertheless, some nuts have "good" fat that can help improve cholesterol ratios.

A Deadly Combination

The formula for good health is not as simple as just getting the correct percentages of carbohydrates, fats, and proteins. You also need a whole host of vitamins and minerals. For example, vitamins A and C are important for your immune system. The B vitamins

Text-Dependent Questions:

1. What is a Calorie?
2. What is a basal metabolic rate (BMR)?
3. What is the unhealthiest form of fat?

are important for your vision, cardiovascular health, energy, and mood. Vitamin D helps the body metabolize phosphorous and calcium, two minerals that are necessary for strong bones. Without the mineral iron, your blood can't carry oxygen to your cells. Vitamin and mineral deficiencies can cause fatigue, weakness, bone loss, illness, and numerous other problems. Vegetables (especially dark leafy greens like kale, spinach, and chard) and fruits, in addition to being a good source of fiber and healthy carbohydrates, are some of your best sources of vitamins and minerals. When it comes to fruits and vegetables, you can't get too many. Yet most American diets are low in fruits and vegetables (especially vegetables!). Instead, when we're hungry, many of us tend to go for foods that we like, are convenient, and fill us up but don't actually have the nutrients we need. Many of these foods are packed with empty Calories.

America's epidemic of girth is ample evidence that we consume more Calories than we burn off. Over the last 20 years, portion sizes have doubled, like soft drink that have increased in size by 52 percent. But surplus Calories may not be the result of simply overeating. An increasingly sedentary lifestyle is another factor. More and more of us are spending greater amounts of time in our cars or in front of computers and televisions. Maybe our minds and fingers get a workout, but little else. To be healthy, your body *needs* exercise as much as any food, vitamin, or mineral. Unfortunately, few Americans get their daily dose of this essential "nutrient."

The technologies that make life convenient also contribute to the problem. People drive short distances instead of walking or ride elevators instead

Research Project

Do some math! Using the formulas on page 47, determine what your BMR is. Next, keep a journal of all your activities during a day, as well as everything you eat. Don't leave anything out, no matter how small! Go online to find one of the many calorie counters on the Internet and use it to figure out how many calories you are using up through exercise. Add this to your BMR. Next, figure out how many calories you are taking in with the food you eat. Compare these two numbers. Do they balance out? If you wanted to lose weight, what would you need to do? How about if you wanted to gain weight?

of taking the stairs. Kids do e-research instead of carrying books home from the library, and we shop online instead of hoofing it up and down the mall. Plus, who cooks anymore? Quick, overprocessed, nutrient-poor but Calorie-rich fast and frozen foods grace our tables much more easily than unprocessed fresh foods. Each of these elements supports excess Calories over time and begins to alter our health. So, it's the combination of Americans' less-than-healthy diet *and* widespread inactivity that's mainly responsible for the obesity epidemic, not just overeating.

Now that you understand what your body needs to be healthy, and what behaviors are contributing to the obesity epidemic, let's take a closer look at all those products and programs the diet industry promotes as "cures" to overweight and obesity. As we look at diets and weight-loss products, remember, the key question is not: *Will this make me lose weight?* The real question is: *Will this make me healthy?*

Words to Understand

trace: Small amounts.
regulatory: An agency that enforces the rules and regulations surrounding something.
copious: Extremely large amounts of something.

Chapter 5

The Quick Fix:
The Skinny
on Diets

- Meal-Replacement Programs
- "Miracle" Products
- Fad Diets

In today's world of fast food, busy schedules, automobiles, office jobs, and sedentary entertainment (like television and computers), living a healthy lifestyle is hard. Being healthy takes effort every single day, the rewards don't appear overnight, and the results won't make you look like a supermodel. That's why diets are so popular. Diets promise a quick fix to our weight woes without the effort or time commitment of living a truly healthy lifestyle. Furthermore, many diets advertise themselves as a way to achieve a supermodel body. So, do these diets deliver? Let's take a look.

Meal-Replacement Programs

To begin our diet discussion, let's talk about some of the most popular diets: meal-replacement programs. In these programs, dieters replace one, two, or even three meals a day with a shake, bar, or specific food. Perhaps the best-known meal-replacement program is Slim-Fast, but there are countless similar products out there. These diets are usually marketed on their simplicity, convenience, and taste. Replace one, two, or three meals a day with the "delicious" chosen product, and watch the pounds melt away.

So, do people lose weight on these programs? Yes, many people do. But are the programs a solution to overweight and obesity, and do they make people healthier? The answer is a resounding no. Here's why.

Meal-replacement programs are in essence starvation diets. Furthermore, there is nothing special about the foods sold for these programs (except that they are expensive). Any weight loss achieved by a meal-replacement program could be achieved regardless of what you replace your meals with. You could replace two meals a day with a bowl of cereal (as some cereal companies now suggest), a hard-boiled egg, or even a candy bar, and you would still achieve weight loss. Why is this? Because there is nothing special about those diet shakes and bars. Even though many of them claim

to be scientifically engineered to increase metabolism, burn fat, and do many other beneficial-sounding things, the truth is that any weight loss a person achieves is based solely on a reduction in his overall caloric intake. Remember our discussion of Calories in chapter 4? After just a few days of negative caloric balance (using more Calories than you consume), a person begins losing weight because her body dips into her fat reserves for the energy it needs. Burning fat is not the result of some expensive miracle shake; it's just what your body does to survive.

Think about it. If your diet shake contains 200 Calories, you drink it for breakfast and lunch, eat no snacks, and then have a "sensible" dinner (let's say of 700 Calories), at the end of the day, you will have consumed only 1,100

Calories—far below what the average body needs. If you replaced all three meals with your shake, you would only consume 600 Calories over the course of the day (a dangerously low sum). Even if you were to eat a snack (let's say of 200 Calories), you would still end the day with a negative caloric balance. Now consider what would happen if you replaced those meals with a candy bar; we'll use Snickers as our example. A regular size (2.1 oz) Snickers bar has 280 Calories. Eat one for breakfast, another for lunch, then eat a 700-Calorie dinner, and your total Calorie intake for the day would be 1,260—still far below what the average person needs. If you kept this negative caloric balance up for just a few days, you would begin losing weight. The reason is simple: You would be starving yourself.

Even though weight may initially be lost on meal-replacement diets, it will inevitably be gained back (and likely a few pounds more). These starvation diets do nothing to address the eating and lifestyle habits or medical condition that brought on the overweight or obesity in the first place. Then they leave participants chronically hungry. Hunger is a basic and powerful instinct. It prevents malnutrition and starvation by prompting the urge to eat. When that urge remains unmet, the body triggers survival mechanisms that work against fat loss. Metabolism slows to conserve energy. The body taps into lean mass for energy in a desperate attempt to cling to fat reserves, which it needs to ward off starvation. Even if body weight decreases, that loss could be almost exclusively in lean mass. In this case, the individual actually becomes fatter (even if she does not become heavier).

People can't stay on these meal-replacement diets forever. How could they? They'd starve to death. Either people give up because they are sick of drinking shakes, eating bars, and being hungry, or they end the program when they've lost the desired amount of weight. Either way, people return to old habits and tend to overeat to compensate for lost Calories. Because lean mass was lost during the diet, and lean mass demands more energy than fat, the dieter now needs fewer Calories per day to function. If her previous lifestyle resulted in chronic surpluses of Calories, now it's even more excessive, and the weight comes back in force.

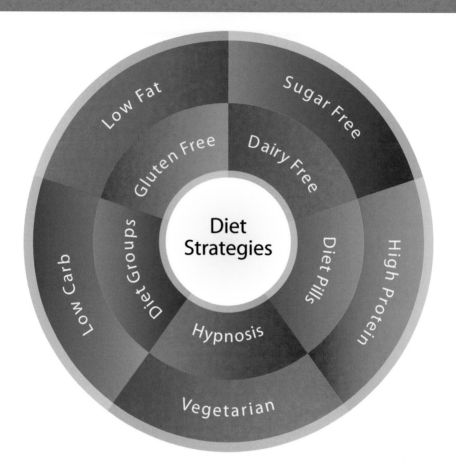

But even if weight did not bounce back after meal-replacement dieting (which it does) these diets would still not make you healthy for a very simple reason; they lack all kinds of essential nutrients. Yes, most diet shakes and bars have vitamins and minerals added, but they are no substitute for the nutrients you get from eating a wide variety of real food. Furthermore, there are plenty of things these replacements don't have, like the fiber so essential to your health, **trace** vitamins and minerals, and other important compounds.

In fact, many diet shakes are little more than powdered milk, sugar or a sugar substitute, added vitamins and minerals, and a thickening agent to make the shake taste creamy and make you feel fuller. You would be getting the same nutrients from drinking a glass of milk and taking a multi-vitamin—something any physician would tell you is not adequate for your body's needs. Many diet bars are the same; they are little more than a candy bar with added vitamins and minerals. These shakes and bars may appeal to one's sweet tooth, but they don't give the body what it needs.

Finally, remember what we said in chapter 4 about exercise? Overweight and obesity are not just caused by eating too much; they are also caused by moving too little. Meal-replacement diets certainly don't do anything by way of exercise. In fact, the drastic reduction in Calories means that you have so much less energy, you may not even be able to perform your normal activities, let alone increase your activity level. Meal-replacement programs, like so many diets, are filled with empty promises. They promise a quick, easy, effortless solution to weight problems. In the end, however, these programs do nothing to make a person healthier (even if a temporary weight loss is achieved) and give no long-term solution to overweight and obesity.

"Miracle" Products

Meal-replacement programs certainly aren't the only products out there promising a quick and effortless road to weight loss. Another very popular form of dieting is by using diet pills, herbal supplements, and other "miracle" products. Some of these products are prescription-only medications, meaning they are drugs you can get only from a doctor. Most of these products, however, are available over-the-counter, meaning anyone can buy them at a pharmacy, grocery, or health-food store.

Different diet pills and supplements work in different ways and to varying degrees. Some are appetite suppressants—they stifle your hunger making it easier for you to eat less. Other products claim to increase your metabolism rate, thereby increasing the number of Calories you burn. Still others claim to chemically interact with fat, making pounds simply melt away.

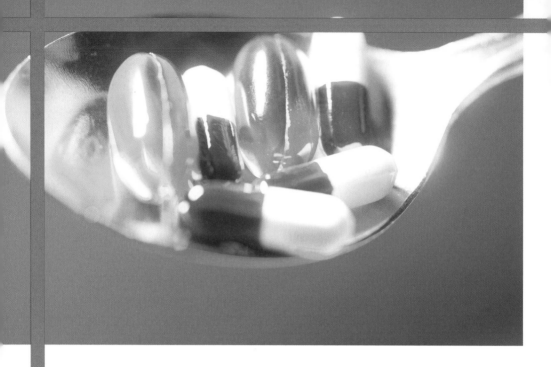

So what do you need to know about this type of diet product? There is no weight-loss miracle, and any product that claims to be one is lying. Some diet pills do contain stimulants like caffeine that can speed up your metabolism for a time, but studies show that these energy spikes don't make any significant contribution to weight loss. Furthermore, no pill can burn your fat or Calories. Only you can do that. Some prescription weight-loss medications do suppress appetite and make it easier for dieters to stick to their diets and lose weight. These prescriptions can be helpful in the short term, especially for people whose obesity has reached such a level that their health or lives are at immediate risk, or for those whose weight does not make more healthy forms of weight loss, especially exercise, possible. But patients aren't meant to stay on these prescriptions (many of which can have serious and unpleasant side effects, including addiction) forever. As is the case with most diets, eventually the dieter must end the program. Usually he returns to the same lifestyle and eating habits that brought on weight gain in the first place and with the same results.

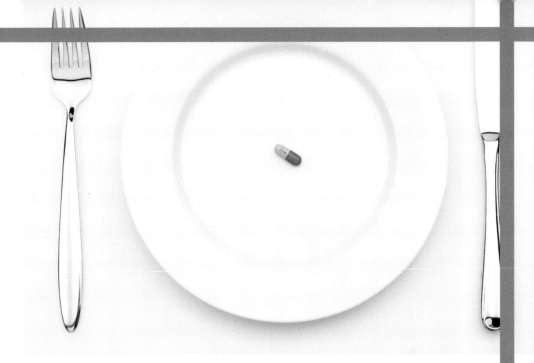

The most important thing to remember about diet pills, herbal supplements, and so-called miracle products however is that many of them are completely unsafe. Over the years, the Food and Drug Administration (FDA), the government **regulatory** body responsible for overseeing food and drug safety in the United States, has pulled numerous diet pills and weight-loss products from the market. These products have caused everything from liver damage, to heart damage, to death. Recent examples include diet pills containing ephedra, which raises blood pressure, stresses the circulatory system, and may increase the risk of heart attack and stroke; herbal supplements and pills containing kava, which can damage the liver; and the popular diet drug fenfluramine, which has been linked to sometimes-fatal heart damage.

Many dieters, though aware of the risks of diet pills, continue to live under the mistaken impression that herbal supplements, because they are "natural," are completely safe. This is untrue. Like any other substance, herbs contain chemicals, and some of those chemicals can be dangerous. Just because something comes from an all-natural source doesn't mean it is safe.

Make Connections:
Food Additive Miracles?

In 1996, the FDA approved a fat substitute, olestra, for use in savory snack foods like potato chips and crackers. At first, many in the public were thrilled. Olestra promised to give foods the same rich flavor normal fat would give, but add no additional fat or Calories. The reason was that olestra, a chemically engineered "fat," could not be absorbed through the intestinal wall and would therefore pass out of the body. It sounded like a miracle product. A person could eat a whole bag of potato chips and not ingest a single gram of fat!

But there are concerns about olestra—it can interfere with your body's absorption of vitamins A, D, E, K and other fat-soluble nutrients. Olestra can also do bad things in the digestive tract. Side effects have included cramping, bloating, excess gas, and loose stools.

Although the FDA and olestra manufacturers maintain the product is safe for human consumption, it may be wise to do your research before digging into those fat-free potato chips. Olestra is usually marketed under the brand name Olean.

Fad Diets

Over the years, there have been plenty of fad diets out there. They rise to popularity seemingly overnight, sometimes gathering thousands of followers, and then fizzle out just as fast. Like many other diet programs, these fad diets usually promise a quick, easy, and miraculous fix to weight-loss problems. Just follow the rules of the diet, and watch the numbers on the scale fall.

Fad diets are no different than the other diets we have discussed so far. They gain huge popularity because they promise miracles. Thousands of people, desperate for a solution to their rising weight, latch onto the empty promises. Eventually these dieters realize the fad is a fraud, and the diet falls into obscurity as quickly as it rose to celebrity. In the end, even those who do

achieve weight loss on such fads will gain the weight back once the diet is over.

One of the most well-known fad diets over the years has been the grapefruit diet. Immensely popular in the 1980s, numerous versions of the diet sprang up. Some claimed you could eat anything you wanted in whatever amounts you desired; as long as you preceded everything you ate with a serving of grapefruit or grapefruit juice, you would lose weight. Other grapefruit diets gave strict meal plans (each meal beginning with grapefruit or grapefruit juice) that had to be followed exactly. Each version of the diet, however, was based on the claim that grapefruit had an almost-magical ability to burn

Make Connections:
A Typical Cabbage Soup Diet

Day 1: Unlimited cabbage soup, unlimited fruit (except bananas), and unlimited water and unsweetened fruit juice.

Day 2: Unlimited cabbage soup, unlimited vegetables, unlimited water (but no juice), and one potato with a dab of butter.

Day 3: Unlimited cabbage soup, unlimited fruit, unlimited vegetables (but no bananas or potatoes), and unlimited water and unsweetened fruit juice.

Day 4: Unlimited cabbage soup, up to eight bananas, and unlimited water and skim milk.

Day 5: Unlimited cabbage soup, up to 20 ounces of beef, up to six tomatoes, and unlimited water.

Day 6: Unlimited cabbage soup, unlimited beef and vegetables (except potatoes), and unlimited water.

Day 7: Unlimited cabbage soup, unlimited brown rice and vegetables (except potatoes), and unlimited water and unsweetened fruit juice.

Research Project

Many people are willing to take drastic measures in order to lose weight. Use the Internet to make a list of some of these. Include strange diet plans, as well as "miracle pills." Find out what the health effects are of each—and tell your class what you've learned.

fat, and by eating grapefruit with every meal, the dieter stimulated her body to burn off extra pounds.

Strikingly similar to the grapefruit diet is the cabbage soup diet. Many different versions of this diet exist as well, but all of them are based on consuming **copious** amounts of cabbage soup. The typical cabbage soup diet has a strict seven-day plan and promises that by the end of the week the dieter will have lost ten or more pounds.

So, do the grapefruit and cabbage soup diets work? As you probably guessed, the answer is no. Certainly many people who follow a grapefruit-diet or cabbage soup-diet meal plan will lose weight, but the reason has nothing to do with the magical properties of grapefruit or cabbage soup. These diets, like meal-replacement programs, are starvation diets. The meal plans are extremely low Calorie. At the end of the day, just about any dieter who adheres to one of these meal plans will have a negative caloric balance and would eventually lose weight. But, as with all the diets we've discussed in this chapter, a person cannot live indefinitely on one of these fad diets. Eventually the diet will end, and any weight that was lost will almost certainly be regained.

Besides being so low Calorie as to be unhealthy, fad diets often have other nutritionally suspect aspects. For example, in our cabbage soup diet, day 1

Text-Dependent Questions:

1. Explain why "natural" does not necessarily mean safe.
2. What is a "fad diet"?
3. What is wrong with most fad diets?

calls for all the fruit and unsweetened fruit juice you desire. Fruit is good for you and provides many nutrients, but where is your protein, your essential fat, your calcium? Plus, unlimited quantities of fruit and juice could send your blood-sugar levels rocketing, forcing your body into insulin-production overdrive. Day 2 calls for unlimited vegetables. That's good for your fiber and many vitamins and minerals (a person can't eat too many vegetables), but what about the other things your body needs? But this certainly isn't the worst of it. Day 5 allows for up to 20 ounces of beef! The United States Department of Agriculture (USDA) recommends a serving of protein to be between 5 and 7 ounces, and that you eat a variety of foods from the Protein Foods Group (this includes sources like chicken, fish, eggs, nuts, or legumes—not just from red meat) each week. On day 5 of the cabbage soup diet, however, you could consume nearly seven servings of beef, a meat that is high in fat and cholesterol! Fad diets simply aren't recipes for good health.

The quick-fix diets, however, are not the only weight-loss programs out there. Today, more and more people realize that weight loss is a long-term goal, and plenty of programs have sprung up promising to be long-term solutions to overweight and obesity. These programs focus on changing long-term habits, adopting new ways of eating and living to achieve weight loss. But do these lifestyle programs have any more to offer than the quick-fix diets, or in the end are they also empty promises?

Words to Understand

hormone: A chemical in the body that has a regulatory or stimulatory effect on something else.

alleged: Claimed to be true, but no evidence has been cited.

leach: To take away slowly.

antithesis: The complete opposite of something.

Chapter 6

From Counting Calories to Cutting Carbs: The Pros and Cons of Lifestyle Programs

- A Mathematician's Dream: Counting Calories

- The Low-Carb Wave

- Living the Low-Fat Lifestyle

The traditional meal-replacement programs, diet pills, fad diets, and other so-called miracle cures certainly aren't the only programs out there promising solutions to overweight and obesity. There are also numerous lifestyle programs. Lifestyle programs are different from traditional diets in that they recognize there are no quick fixes to weight issues. They advocate adopting new eating habits and lifestyles as permanent solutions to weight loss. The specific changes called for, however, vary drastically from program to program. Sometimes two programs even recommend completely opposite ways of eating, yet both promise to be permanent weight-loss solutions. Also unlike traditional diets, most lifestyle programs claim to be not just roads to weight loss, but also roads to good health. And are they? Let's take a closer look at some of today's most popular lifestyle programs.

A Mathematician's Dream: Counting Calories

According to many lifestyle programs, the key to weight loss is Calorie counting. This makes a lot of common sense. Remember our previous Calorie discussions? We've said over and over that weight gain and weight loss rely on simple formulas: more Calories taken in than used = weight gain; more Calories used than taken in = weight loss.

Calorie-counting lifestyle programs are self-explanatory. In them, dieters determine how many Calories they can eat in a day and still lose weight, keep track of the caloric value of everything they eat, and make sure that by the end of each day they have eaten only the number of Calories allowed. If the dieter can stick to the program, she will lose weight.

There are only two problems with Calorie counting. The first is that it is extremely difficult. It requires knowing the exact number of Calories in every food you eat. This isn't so hard for, let's say, a handful of crackers. In that case you can just look on the box's nutrition label, calculate how many

Calories are in each cracker, and multiply that number by the number of crackers you are going to eat. It gets more difficult, however, for foods that don't come with nutrition labels, like an apple or a serving of squash. Start mixing foods together, like making a sandwich with bread, a smear of mustard, turkey, lettuce, tomato, sprouts, and sliced onions, and things start getting really difficult!

Because Calorie counting is hard and can make you feel like you're doing mathematical somersaults, many people seek help along the way, and there are plenty of programs out there ready to provide their services. Calorie-counting dieters may buy books that give the Calorie contents for numerous foods; they may join clubs that exchange Calorie-counting recipes; they may buy prepackaged meals that have all the Calorie counting done for them, and they may join programs (like Weight Watchers® for example) that simplify the Calorie-counting process through point systems. Buying products or joining clubs to make Calorie counting easier is not necessarily a bad thing, but it can be extremely expensive. Not everyone who needs to lose weight or wants to be healthy can afford such conveniences, and if left to juggle the

mathematics on their own, many Calorie-counting dieters eventually give up and return to old eating habits.

The second concern in Calorie-counting lifestyle programs is that Calorie counting alone may help you lose weight, but it will not necessarily make you healthy. Let's say you have determined (through calculating your BMR, physical activity, and thermic effect of food as discussed in chapter 4) that your body needs 1,900 Calories a day. Perhaps you've been eating 2,400 Calories on a regular basis and have therefore been gaining weight. If you cut back to 1,900 Calories, you will lose weight. But if those 1,900 Calories come just from ice cream and potato chips, you will not be healthy because you won't be giving your body the nutrients it needs. When considering a Calorie-counting lifestyle program, it is absolutely essential for people to remember that, while weight loss can result from simply cutting the *quantity* of food, to be healthy one needs to eat the right *quality* of food. Furthermore, for many people, cutting Calories shouldn't be the only answer to health and weight loss. Increasing exercise is just as important.

Frustrated with the complications of counting Calories, many people turn to lifestyle programs that dictate not precisely *how much* food one can eat but what *kinds* of food contribute to weight gain or loss. The change in focus from quantity to quality has given rise to all kinds of new lifestyle programs, among them low-fat diets and low-carb diets. Let's begin by talking about the newest craze, the low-carb diet.

The Low-Carb Wave

Today, you are probably hearing a lot about low-carbohydrate diets. They're all the rage. The Atkins Nutritional Approach™ is, of course, the best known of these programs, but there are many others out there, and all are based on a single theory: Carbohydrates are the root of America's overweight and obesity epidemic, and by cutting carbohydrates, one can lose weight and keep it off. The programs offer a range of explanations for carbohydrates' fat-packing power (some more scientific than others). The most common explanation of carbohydrates' dangers hinges on insulin, the **hormone** that regulates the amount of sugar in your blood.

As we discussed in chapter 4, all carbohydrates are sugars. As your body digests the carbohydrates, sugar is released into your bloodstream. The sugar's presence triggers your pancreas to secrete insulin, which picks up the sugar molecules and carries them into your cells where they get "burned" for energy. If you have too much sugar in your blood, however, your cells won't be able to burn the fuel fast enough and will store the sugar as fat. If these sugar-floods happen too often, your cells may build a resistance to insulin, a situation that increases one's risk of developing diabetes.

Proponents of low-carbohydrate diets (as well as some recent medical studies) claim that insulin plays an important role in regulating appetite. According to the theory, if insulin receptors in the brain are working properly, you will feel appropriate hunger or fullness in response to what you eat. If the receptors become resistant to insulin, however, you will continue feeling hungry even when you are actually full. What results is constant craving (mostly for carbohydrates), in essence, carbohydrate "addiction."

Carbohydrates' **alleged** addictive power leaves us with a problem. Your body burns glucose (a form of sugar) for energy, and carbohydrates are our bodies' main source of glucose. Without carbohydrates, where will our energy come from? Low-carb diets claim to have a solution. By cutting carbs to an extremely low level, you will force your body to burn fat for energy instead of carbohydrates, a process called lipolysis. The vast majority of carbohydrates in a person's diet are replaced with protein. On low-carb diets, therefore, all the foods that conventional wisdom and science tell us are healthy and should be eaten plentifully (fruits, vegetables, and whole grains) are suspect and limited. All the foods we've learned should be consumed in limited or even spare quantities (meat-based proteins and fats) are eaten liberally.

Low-carbohydrate programs usually rely on stages. The first stage requires severely restricting carbohydrates to kick-start lipolysis. (The Atkins program, for example, begins with a two-week phase called Induction in which carbohydrates are cut to fewer than 20 grams a day; no fruits, grains, legumes, starchy vegetables, or other "high-carb" foods are allowed; and meat and fat are eaten plentifully.) Once weight loss is under way, the dieter can add carbohydrates back into his diet a little at a time. If weight loss stops or weight gain starts, the dieter backtracks to a previous low-carb stage. After the dieter reaches his desired weight, he finds the amount of carbohydrates he can eat in a day without losing or gaining weight, and maintains that diet for the rest of his life.

So do low-carb diets work, and can they make you healthy? So far, the reviews are mixed. The theories on which the low-carb craze is based have yet to be scientifically proven or disproved—whether carbohydrates actually cause addiction, therefore, is still in question. Whether or not these theories are correct, some recent studies have shown that low-carb diets can cause

According to the Atkins Nutritional Approach, the average person will need to eat between 60 and 90 grams of carbohydrates each day to maintain his current weight over his lifetime. That's approximately 190 to 210 fewer grams each day than the Group Health Cooperate recommends for people eating a 2,000 Calorie diet!

significant weight loss, something most dieters are happy to hear. However, in 2009, in a study published in the *New England Journal of Medicine* found that after two years participants that were on a low-carb diet and those that were on a higher-carb diet lost the same amount of weight by restricting calories. It was not the cutting of carbs, but the cutting of calories that caused the weight loss.

Yes, low-carb diets can cause weight loss, at least initially, but like all the diets we have discussed so far, long-term health and weight management are still big issues. First of all, low-carb lifestyles are relatively new, and the long-term risks are still unknown. Based on what we know about the human body and its nutritional needs, however, we can make some educated guesses about what those risks might be.

Most low-carb programs tend to lump all carbohydrates together. As we discussed in chapter 4, not all carbohydrates are the same. Simple carbohydrates (like the ones found in white bread or in your sugar bowl) lack many nutrients and just give your body empty Calories, so cutting simple carbohydrates from your life can be perfectly healthy. But don't throw the baby out with the bathwater! Complex carbohydrates have all kinds of nutrients that are essential to your health. They are also a great source of fiber, which as we've learned not only helps out in the digestive tract but also protects against conditions like heart disease and colon cancer. No amount of protein or fat can give you all the nutrients and fiber you need. Most low-carb lifestyle programs claim you can still get your vitamins, minerals, and fiber while eating drastically reduced carbohydrates. But think about it, if you are supposed to get 20 to 35 grams of fiber each day, but your low-carb lifestyle only allows for 15 grams of carbohydrates, where is that fiber going to come from? In reality, most people cannot get all their nutrients on such a strict dietary regime. Furthermore, with fewer carbohydrates, low-carb dieters may find they have less energy for exercise, which we know is essential to good health.

Replacing carbohydrates with protein is another problem in low-carb programs. Low-carb/high-protein diets also tend to be high-fat diets. There are many low-fat sources of protein in the world; unfortunately for low-carb dieters, most of those sources come from plants, contain carbohydrates, and are therefore forbidden or strictly limited by the lifestyle program. What protein sources are left? Meat and animal products, many of which are high in saturated fat and cholesterol. While many low-carb dieters find it easier to cut the overall amount of food they eat in a day by filling up on protein and fat, there may be serious consequences (like an increased risk of heart disease or colon cancer) down the road. Furthermore, a gram of fat has more than twice the Calories of a gram of carbohydrate, so at the end of the day it's easy to consume more Calories even if you've eaten less food.

A further concern about high-protein diets is that your body can only use so much protein at once. Some of the protein goes to repairing your tissues, some gets converted to sugar and burned for energy, and the rest gets flushed from your body. Some doctors fear that this cleansing process may

**Make Connections:
The Glycemic Index**

According to the Harvard School of Public Health, the carbohydrate story may be even more complicated than separating carbs into "simple" and "complex." Simple carbohydrates are generally considered bad because they trigger a quick rise in blood-sugar levels. As Harvard researchers point out, however, not all simple carbohydrates actually cause such a rise. Many types of fruit, for example, contain simple carbohydrates but are also high in fiber and are therefore digested more slowly. Similarly, a high-fat food containing simple carbohydrates (like ice cream) will also be broken down more slowly, resulting in a gradual rise rather than a spike in blood sugar. The Harvard School of Public Health suggests that people judge carbohydrates not in terms of simple or complex but according to something called the glycemic index. The glycemic index rates foods by their effect on blood sugar. High-glycemic foods (like potatoes and white bread) make blood sugar spike. Low-glycemic foods (like most legumes, whole fruits, and whole wheat) cause a more gradual increase in blood-sugar levels.

leach calcium from your bones and stress your kidneys. Since no long-term studies have been done on low-carb/high-protein diets, we have yet to see if this will be a significant danger.

Finally, like all of the diets we've discussed so far, the low-carb lifestyle is almost impossible for most people to stick to long term. Even if there were no long-term health risks (which there very well might be), the effort it takes to count every last gram of carbohydrate and the extremely limited food options available on a low-carb diet practically guarantee that most people will eventually give up the diet and return to their old habits. Once they do, they will almost certainly regain the weight they lost. But low-carb diets, though currently hugely popular, are definitely not the only lifestyle programs out there. Let's take a look at another popular lifestyle program, the low-fat diet, to see how it stacks up.

Living the Low-Fat Lifestyle

Although currently falling in popularity to low-carb diets, for years low-fat lifestyle programs were what the doctor ordered to combat overweight and obesity. Immensely popular just a decade ago, these programs now struggle against Atkins-crazed sensibilities. Just the thought of cutting back on meat, chicken, and fish smacks of heresy, and *increase* carbs? Unthinkable! But is such skepticism warranted? Let's take a closer look.

Interestingly, low-fat lifestyle programs are the exact **antithesis** of low-carb programs. On low-fat programs, you can eat lots of carbohydrates (although most low-fat programs do advocate cutting sugar consumption) but must drastically reduce fat intake. The theory behind these programs is that your body burns carbohydrates more readily than fat. Fat, therefore, is more likely to be stored than burned, contributing to weight gain. If you eliminate fat, you eliminate the major storage material and a huge Calorie contributor from your diet, and weight loss follows.

Low-fat diets make sense on the surface and have many benefits. By switching to low-fat foods like vegetables and fruits, you increase your intake of nutrients and fiber. By cutting saturated fat from your diet, you cut cholesterol. By increasing fiber and decreasing cholesterol, you lower your risk of developing conditions like heart disease and colon cancer.

Low-fat diets can be extremely healthy. The problem is that many people go about low-fat diets in the wrong way. Interestingly, the trappings of low-fat diets are very similar to the problems with low-carb diets. Just like low-carb diets, low-fat lifestyle programs tend to lump all carbohydrates and all fats into the same category. The result is that many low-fat dieters assume that any food that is low in fat or fat free is perfectly safe to eat and end up replacing their fat Calories with empty simple-carbohydrate Calories.

health

Similarly, they assume that any food containing fat is bad and end up cutting even healthy fats from their diets.

To make matters worse, plenty of companies have jumped on the low-fat bandwagon promising healthy fare that is really just potential weight gain in disguise. What do two tablespoons of regular-fat peanut butter and two tablespoons of *reduced*-fat peanut butter have in common? According to the NIH, they both have 190 Calories. How many fewer Calories does a half cup of *non*fat ice cream have than a half cup of regular ice cream? According to the same source, only ten (180 and 190 respectively). Some low-fat dieters even wolf down entire bags of cookies, candies, and pretzels in one sitting, all because marketers stamp "low fat" on packaging. Moviegoers inhale boxes of Mike and Ike's, but pass on buttered popcorn. It's no wonder people aren't successful losing weight! If you remember nothing more, remember this: Just because a food claims to be low fat doesn't mean it's low Calorie. Even if you cut fat from your diet, if you continue consuming more Calories than you burn, you will keep gaining weight.

Like the other diets and lifestyle programs we have discussed, low-fat lifestyles can also be very difficult to stick to. Fat tastes good and is very satisfying to eat. When you can't get any, you may find yourself eating more of other foods in an attempt to fill up and banish the craving, a tendency that

Make Connections: Fat Tricks

Did you ever wonder what the difference is between low-fat mayo and reduced-fat mayo? According to the FDA, food manufacturers cannot use any of the following terms to describe a product unless that product meets the criteria defined below:

Fat free = less than 0.5 grams of fat per serving
Low fat = less than or equal to 3 grams of fat
Reduced fat = at least 25 percent less fat than traditional version

Note: A fat-free food, then, can really have up to 1/2 gram of fat, and a reduced-fat item may not be low fat at all!

results in consuming more total Calories. Even if their willpower holds for a time, most low-fat dieters still can't stick to the plan for the long term. And once they return to their old lifestyle habits, they will regain their weight.

Text-Dependent Questions:

1. What are two problems with calorie-counting?
2. List three problems with low-carb diets.
3. What is the glycemic index?

Research Project

Pick one of the diet plans described in this chapter and find out more about it. Use the library or the Internet to discover the answers to these questions: What is the history behind this plan? Who created it? How long has it been around? Have scientists done any studies on it to prove or disprove whether it can help with weight loss? What are the possible side effects or dangers involved with diet? What are the possible advantages? Put your answers together into a written or oral report.

Despite the confusion, difficulties, and misleading products surrounding low-fat lifestyle programs, today most doctors still recommend a low-fat diet combined with exercise as the best treatment for overweight and obesity and the surest road to good health. Anyone who wishes to embark on a low-fat lifestyle program, however, must remember that just because he's cutting fat doesn't mean he can fill up on empty Calories. The surest road to good health is not by living according to one mantra like "fat is bad." It's by understanding all of your nutritional and exercise needs and then meeting those needs every day.

Words to Understand

 empowered: Having a sense of self-confidence or self-esteem.

Chapter 7

Tipping the Scale: Learning to Separate Fact and Fiction

- No Weight-Loss Miracles

- Setting the Right Goals

- Separating Fact and Fiction

No Weight-Loss Miracles

In the last two chapters, we've examined numerous diets and lifestyle programs and learned that all of them have failings. Some are plain unhealthy, even dangerous. Others are filled with empty promises. Still others, even if highly beneficial, are simply too difficult for most people to stick to long term.

As much as it pains us to hear it, there is simply no such thing as a weight-loss miracle. Significant weight gain does not happen overnight. It happens over time as positive caloric balances outnumber negative caloric balances. These positive caloric balances are usually the result of habitually eating too much of the wrong type of food and exercising too little. Similarly, significant weight loss cannot happen overnight. It can only happen when negative caloric balances outnumber positive caloric balances over time, and when the eating and lifestyle habits that led to the weight gain are corrected.

Setting the Right Goals

Of course many people in America want to and should lose weight. But basing one's goals exclusively on weight loss can be unhealthy and counterproductive. Overweight and obesity certainly carry serious health risks, but losing weight can carry risks of its own. If one goes about losing weight in the wrong way, she can do further damage to her health and alter her body so that it's even more difficult to lose weight in the future. Furthermore, if a person's only goal is weight loss and she doesn't see the desired results in a certain amount of time, she can easily become frustrated, give up her attempts completely,

and return to the unhealthy lifestyle that brought on overweight or obesity in the first place.

Living a healthy lifestyle is never easy (that's why so few of us actually live healthy lifestyles). The first step is to ask yourself what you want. Are you trying to look like a rail-thin supermodel? If your answer is yes, where did you get the idea that you should look this way? Does anyone you know look like this? Maybe the emaciated look is someone else's idea of success, but what should your idea of success be?

There are plenty of diets out there that can help you achieve short-term weight loss. Your chances for long-term success, however, will increase greatly if you forget about diets, change your goals, and educate yourself about what your body really needs.

Weight loss alone is not the answer. Becoming healthy is the key, and being healthy should be part of every person's goals—whether or not that person needs to lose weight. If a person truly focuses on improving her health rather than on losing weight, she can make all kinds of changes to her habits—like eating appropriate amounts of healthy foods, cutting out unhealthy foods, and exercising every day—that will be beneficial no matter how much weight she believes she should lose. For a person who is suffering overweight or obesity, these changes will naturally lead to weight loss, but this weight loss will be just one aspect of her improved health and life.

Does Being Healthy Mean I Can Never Enjoy Myself Again?

Many people think that living a healthy lifestyle means never indulging in an "unhealthy" food like potato chips or ice cream again. This is plainly untrue. The "unhealthy" foods you enjoy can be part of a perfectly healthy lifestyle. The key is moderation. You may not be able to eat these foods every day or in large amounts, but the occasional fatty food or sugary indulgence won't derail your goal of good health.

Research Project

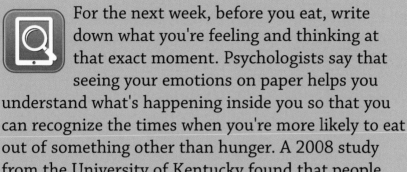

For the next week, before you eat, write down what you're feeling and thinking at that exact moment. Psychologists say that seeing your emotions on paper helps you understand what's happening inside you so that you can recognize the times when you're more likely to eat out of something other than hunger. A 2008 study from the University of Kentucky found that people choose lower-calorie foods when they are aware of their feelings. After doing this for a week, what do you think? Does writing down your feelings help you to eat in a more healthy way?

Separating Fact and Fiction

Now you are armed with some knowledge about what it takes to be healthy. You also know more about all those forces out there saying you need to look a certain way and trying to sell you products to achieve that look. Instead of listening to all those media messages telling you to be thin, take some time to examine and question their messages. Instead of automatically trusting the claims a company makes about its products, ask what evidence they have to support those claims.

So what should you look for when you examine a diet product or program? First and foremost, how does it conform to what you now know about proper nutrition? If the product or program interferes with your ability to get all your vitamins, minerals, nutrients, and necessary exercise, it is not

Text-Dependent Questions:

1. How does weight loss happen?
2. What are five questions to ask when you are evaluating a diet plan?

going to make you healthy (even if it causes a short-term weight loss). Second, does it promise miracles? By now you know that there is no such thing as a weight-loss miracle. If it sounds too good to be true, it is. Third, where is the real science behind the product or program's claims? Advertisers may cite lots of case studies or scientific-sounding evidence to back their claims, but have real doctors reviewed any of these cases or claims? Have studies appeared in medical journals? Are the sources trustworthy? And most important, does the person or group citing the evidence have something (like money) to gain by convincing you of the claims? If you are truly educated about the sources and evidence behind diet claims, you will be less likely to fall for the advertising tricks and pseudoscience the diet industry uses to trap you. If you can't figure out whether a product or program is safe and effective, ask your doctor.

Not every single product or program out there is unhealthy or a waste of time, and you may find certain books, groups, or products that really do help people live healthier lifestyles. But once you have the right goals and understand what it really takes to be healthy, you won't need to rely on the diet industry's products or programs. Feeling **empowered** is the key to achieving success. Not everyone can look like a supermodel, but everyone can strive for good health. So if you find something out there in the diet industry that helps you achieve better health, that's great. But if you don't, there's no need to be discouraged. You don't need the diet industry anyway.

Series Glossary of Key Terms

Aerobic exercise: Activities that use large muscle groups (back, chest, and legs) to increase heart rate and breathing for an extended period of time, such as bicycling, brisk walking, running, and swimming. Federal guidelines recommend that adults get 150 to 300 minutes of aerobic activity a week.

Body mass index (BMI): A measure of body weight relative to height that uses a mathematical formula to get a score to determine if a person is underweight, at a normal weight, overweight, or obese. For adults, a BMI of 18.5 to 24.9 is considered healthy; a person with a BMI of 25 to 29.9 is considered overweight, and a person with a BMI of 30 or more is considered obese. BMI charts for children compare their height and weight to other children of their same sex and age.

Calorie: A unit of energy in food.

Carbohydrate: A type of food that is a major source of energy for your body. Your digestive system changes carbohydrates into blood glucose (sugar). Your body uses this sugar to make energy for cells, tissues, and organs, and stores any extra sugar in your liver and muscles for when it is needed. If there is more sugar than the body can use, it is stored as body fat.

Cholesterol: A fat-like substance that is made by your body and found naturally in animal foods such as dairy products, eggs, meat, poultry, and seafood. Foods high in cholesterol include dairy fats, egg yolks, and organ meats such as liver. Cholesterol is needed to carry out functions such as hormone and vitamin production, but too much can build up inside arteries, increasing the risk of heart disease.

Diabetes: A person with this disease has blood glucose—sugar—levels that are above normal levels. Insulin is a hormone that helps the glucose get into your cells to give them energy. Diabetes occurs when the body does not make enough insulin or does not use the insulin it makes. Over time, having too much sugar in your blood may cause serious problems. It may damage your eyes, kidneys, and nerves, and may cause heart disease and stroke. Regular physical activity, weight control, and healthy eating helps to control or prevent diabetes.

Diet: What a person eats and drinks. It may also be a type of eating plan.

Fat: A major source of energy in the diet that also helps the body absorb fat-soluble vitamins, such as vitamins A, D, E, and K.

High blood pressure: Blood pressure refers to the way blood presses against the blood vessels as it flows through them. With high blood pressure, the heart works harder, and the chances of a stroke, heart attack, and kidney problems are greater.

Metabolism: The process that occurs in the body to turn the food you eat into energy your body can use.

Nutrition: The process of the body using food to sustain life.

Obesity: Excess body fat that is more than 20 percent of what is considered to be healthy.

Overweight: Excess body fat that is more than 10 to 20 percent of what is considered to be healthy.

Portion size: The amount of a food served or eaten in one occasion. A portion is not a standard amount (it's different from a "serving size"). The amount of food it includes may vary by person and occasion.

Protein: One of the nutrients in food that provides calories to the body. Protein is an essential nutrient that helps build many parts of the body, including blood, bone, muscle, and skin. It is found in foods like beans, dairy products, eggs, fish, meat, nuts, poultry, and tofu.

Saturated fat: This type of fat is solid at room temperature. It is found in foods like full-fat dairy products, coconut oil, lard, and ready-to-eat meats. Eating a diet high in saturated fat can raise blood cholesterol and increase the risk of heart disease.

Serving size: A standard amount of a food, such as a cup or an ounce.

Stroke: When blood flow to your brain stops, causing brain cells to begin to die.

Trans fats: A type of fat produced when liquid fats (oils) are turned into solid fats through a chemical process called hydrogenation. Eating a large amount of trans fats raises blood cholesterol and increases the risk of heart disease.

Unsaturated fat: These healthier fats are liquid at room temperature. Vegetable oils are a major source of unsaturated fat. Other foods, such as avocados, fatty fish like salmon and tuna, most nuts, and olives are good sources of unsaturated fat.

Whole grains: Grains and grain products made from the entire grain seed; usually a good source of dietary fiber.

Further Reading

Bowden, Johnny. *The 150 Healthiest Foods on Earth: The Surprising, Unbiased Truth About What You Should Eat and Why*. Gloucester: Fair Winds Press, 2007.

Stollman, Lisa. *The Teen Eating Manifesto: The Ten Essential Steps to Losing Weight, Looking Great and Getting Healthy (Volume 1)*. Northport: Nirvana Press, 2012.

Wiatt, Carrie & Barbara Schroeder. *The Diet for Teenagers Only*. New York: HarperCollins Publishers Inc., 2005.

For More Information

Academy of Nutrition and Dietetics
www.eatright.org

Centers for Disease Control and Prevention
www.cdc.gov

Cool Nurse
coolnurse.healthology.com/main/general.aspx

DietFacts
www.dietfacts.com

Diet Information
www.diet-i.com

The Healthy Weight Network
www.healthyweight.net

National Association to Advance Fat Acceptance
www.naafaonline.com/dev2

National Center for Health Statistics
www.cdc.gov/nchs

National Food Laboratory
www.thenfl.com

National Institutes of Health
www.nih.gov

National Library of Medicine
www.nlm.nih.gov

Publisher's note:
The websites listed on this page were active at the time of publication. The publisher is not responsible for websites that have changed their addresses or discontinued operation since the date of publication. The publisher will review and update the website list upon each reprint.

Index

About the Authors & the Consultant

Jean Ford is a freelance author, writer, award-winning illustrator, and public speaker. Internationally recognized, her work includes writing for periodicals from the United States to China, and speaking to audiences from as close as her tri-state area to as far away as Africa. Although she generally writes and speaks on nonfiction topics, Jean also enjoys writing and illustrating children's books.

Autumn Libal received her degree from Smith College in Northampton, MA. A former water-aerobics instructor, she now dedicates herself exclusively to writing for young people. Other Mason Crest series she has contributed to include PSYCHIATRIC DISORDERS: DRUGS & PSYCHOLOGY FOR THE MIND AND BODY, YOUTH WITH SPECIAL NEEDS, and THE SCIENCE OF HEALTH: YOUTH AND WELL-BEING. She has also written health-related articles for *New Moon: The Magazine for Girls and Their Dreams*.

Dr. Victor F. Garcia is the co-director of the Comprehensive Weight Management Center at Cincinnati Children's Hospital Medical Center. He is a board member of Discover Health of Greater Cincinnati, a fellow of the American College of Surgeons, and a two-time winner of the Martin Luther King Humanitarian Award.

Picture Credits